A TALKING POINTS BOOK BY
DAVE GOBBETT

THE ENVIRONMENT

To Sally,
who opened my eyes a little wider to the
beauty of God's creation.

Environment
© David Gobbett, 2022.

Published by:
The Good Book Company

thegoodbook.com | thegoodbook.co.uk
thegoodbook.com.au | thegoodbook.co.nz | thegoodbook.co.in

ISBN: 9781784987916 | Printed in the UK

Design by André Parker

CONTENTS

INTRODUCTION
TALKING POINTS

The world is changing at an astonishing speed.

And not just politics, technology and communication but our whole culture, morality and attitudes. Christians living in Western culture have enjoyed the benefit of being in a world which largely shared our assumptions about what is fundamentally right and wrong. We can no longer assume that this is the case.

In two short generations we have moved to a widespread adoption of liberal values, many of which are in conflict with the teaching of the Bible. Increasingly, believers are finding themselves to be the misunderstood minority and feeling at odds with where the world seems to be heading.

But let's not be short-sighted: some of this change has been good. Christians have often failed to discern the difference between our own cultural values and those that are demanded by Scripture. We are as prone to bigotry as others. We have much to repent of in our attitudes towards, for example, the freedom and role of women in society and our lack of compassion and understanding towards those who have wrestled with same-sex attraction, for example.

Sometimes it's easier to protest and rage against the tide of history than to go back to our Bibles and think carefully about what God is saying—holding up society's views, and our own, to the truth-revealing mirror that is God's word.

At our best, we Christians have been in the forefront of social reform. Think of the great 19th-century reformers of the slave trade, prisons and poverty: William Wilberforce, Elizabeth Fry and Lord Shaftesbury. But too often, we now find ourselves on the back foot, unable to articulate a clear response to a pressing question of our day. And even when we have understood God's mind on a particular issue, we have struggled to apply it compassionately in our speech and in our relationships. Christians are called to be wise and gentle, even when the temptation is to call out injustices and be rightly angry. The way to approach these issues is to prayerfully and humbly seek to understand our culture and discern the times.

This short series of books is an attempt to help ordinary Christians think constructively about a range of issues—moral, ethical and cultural—that run against the grain for those who name Christ as Lord. We want to stimulate believers to talk with each other as we search the Scriptures together. The aim is to help us think biblically, constructively and compassionately, and not to feel intimidated when we are challenged or questioned, or, perhaps worse, remain silent. This book will lend perspective and offers some biblical guidance on following God and loving people as God loves us.

WHAT THIS BOOK IS NOT...

In such a short book, we cannot hope to answer all the questions you may have about how to think about the environment. Nor can we address the many scientific and political debates that are at play, or all the practical decisions that may be facing you personally.

Nor does this book present a thorough treatment of all the Bible has to say on these questions. If that is what you are hungry for, there will be other, longer, and perhaps more technical books that will help you dig deeper.

WHAT THIS BOOK IS...

Rather, our aim is to give you an accessible intro-duction to the many questions that surround the conversation about the environment, as we hold our questions up to the big story of the Bible: the story of creation, fall, redemption and eternity.

But we also hope that this book takes us beyond the issues facing our planet—to a greater worship of the God who made it and a deeper love for those who inhabit it. You may be gravely concerned about the environment; or you may be more sceptical. Whatever your situation, we hope this book will be a first step towards understanding the landscape of this issue, and an encouragement to know and share the love and hope we have in Christ.

Tim Thornborough
Series Editor | June 2022

environment

[uhn-vai-ruh-muhnt]

noun: **environment**

1. The surroundings or conditions in which a person, animal, or plant lives or operates.

2. The natural world, as a whole or in a particular geographical area, especially as affected by human activity.

synonyms: nature, the world, the earth
"the impact of pesticides on the environment"

[Source: Google definitions]

"*My name is Greta Thunberg. I am 16 years old. I come from Sweden. And I want you to panic. I want you to act as if your house was on fire. Because it is ... Our civilization is so fragile it is almost like a castle built in the sand. The facade is so beautiful but the foundations are far from solid. We have been cutting so many corners. Yesterday the world watched with despair and enormous sorrow how Notre-Dame burned in Paris. Some buildings are more than just buildings. But Notre-Dame will be rebuilt. I hope that its foundations are strong. I hope that our foundations are even stronger. But I fear they are not.*"

Greta Thunberg, European Parliament,
Strasbourg, 16th April 2019
No One Is Too Small to Make a Difference,
p 45-46.

GREETING GRETA
CHAPTER ONE

When *Time* magazine chose Greta Thunberg as their person of the year for 2019, it was hard to argue with. The Swedish teenager—whose meteoric rise has seen her address everyone from presidents to popes to the United Nations General Assembly—is a modern-day sensation. More than that, the concerns which she champions look set to shape both our political agendas and our consumer choices for decades to come.

But how have we got here? Where has environmentalism come from? And what should Christians make of it all?

A VERY BRIEF HISTORY OF GREEN

As a cultural phenomenon, the environmental movement is a relatively recent one. Hot on the heels of the Industrial Revolution, hints of a so-called

"Green Romanticism" can be found in the writing of 19th-century poets William Wordsworth and Percy Bysshe Shelley, whose works drew attention to the beauty and importance of nature.[1] Towards the middle of the 20th century, pollution became a growing concern, along with the damage that "acid rain" was causing, leading to the forming of pressure groups (for example, Friends of the Earth in 1969 and Greenpeace in 1971) and political parties (The Green Party of England and Wales in 1990). In 1985 the big news story was the discovery of a hole in the ozone layer, due to the excessive use of chloro-fluorocarbons or CFCs in appliances such as fridges and air-conditioning units. Concepts such as the "greenhouse effect" and "global warming" entered the mainstream. In 2006 awareness was raised still further by the release of former US Vice President Al Gore's documentary, *An Inconvenient Truth*.

Bible-believing Christians can often be slow out of the blocks when it comes to engaging with cultural issues, but as early as 1970 the respected evangelical leader Francis Schaeffer wrote the landmark book *Pollution and the Death of Man*, urging Christians to take seriously their stewardship of creation. In the years that followed, organisations like those

---

1 Lisa Ottum, *Wordsworth and the Green Romantics* (New Hampshire Historical Society, 2016).

associated with *A Rocha* (founded in 1983) have sprung up, which engage in scientific research, environmental education, and community-based conservation projects around the world.[2]

For the last 25 years, the UN Framework Convention on Climate Change (UNFCCC) has organised several significant conferences. In 1997 the Kyoto Protocol was adopted by 192 nations, with the general aim of reducing global greenhouse-gas emissions. This in turn was succeeded, in 2015, by the Paris Agreement, which put specific numbers on paper: namely, a commitment to limiting global temperature rises to less than 2°C, and ideally 1.5°C. In 2021 COP26 gathered in Glasgow, and 151 nations committed to reducing their use of coal, supporting developing countries, and devising plans to slash carbon emissions by 2030 with the stated aim of reaching "net zero" by 2050.

Maybe this all sounds a bit jargony. Perhaps some quick-fire facts and figures will bring things closer to home.

- **The planet is warming.** It took many thousands of years for the earth's temperature to increase by 0.5°C; it has gone up by a further 1°C in the last 100 years alone. This has resulted in melting

---

2 Pronounced "Ah-Rosher", from the Portuguese for "The Rock". See https://www.arocha.org/en/ (accessed 28 March 2022).

ice caps and rising sea levels. By 2100, it is estimated that the world's oceans will have risen by one metre (3.3'). This threatens to devastate whole countries like Bangladesh, where currently 10 million people live below the "one-metre contour".[3]

- **Biodiversity is plummeting.** Around 1.2 million species of plants and animals have been identified by scientists. This vast diversity of living things that call our planet home is not an irrelevance or a luxury, but together with our land, water and air, creates a rich ecosystem that enables sustainable life. According to the International Union for Conservation of Nature, one in four species is at risk of extinction, with a 70% decline in the populations of mammals, birds, fish, reptiles and amphibians since 1970.[4]

- **There is widespread deforestation.** The Amazonian rainforest contains a bewildering half of the world's the living species and acts as an enormous carbon sponge, absorbing vast quantities of CO_2 and converting it into oxygen. However, between 2001 and 2019, Brazil lost to deforestation

---

3 https://www.science.org/content/article/sea-levels-rise-bangladeshi-islanders-must-decide-between-keeping-water-out-or-letting (accessed 28 March 2022).

4 https://www.bbc.co.uk/news/science-environment-58859105 (accessed 28 March 2022).

140 million acres (57 million hectares)—an area larger than the state of California. Throughout 2019 alone, an entire football-field's worth of rainforest was lost to the planet every six seconds.[5]

- **Plastic pollution continues to blight our oceans.** Every minute of every day, the equivalent to a lorry load of plastic is dumped into the sea. And if the current rate continues, by 2050 there will be more plastic in the earth's seas, by weight, than fish.[6]
- **The quality of the earth's soil is deteriorating.** This is the result of aggressive agricultural practices—such as allowing water run-off, the use of nitrogen fertilizers and over-grazing—combined with extreme weather events.[7] The processes that generate the kind of high-quality topsoil that is needed to grow vegetation take centuries, but the world is churning through that soil at a phenomenal rate.[8]

I wonder how you respond to reading all of that? Still sitting comfortably?

---

5 https://www.globalforestwatch.org/blog/data-and-research/global-tree-cover-loss-data-2019/ (accessed 20 March 2022).

6 https://www.independent.co.uk/climate-change/news/ocean-plastic-fish-climate-crisis-sea-study-a9635241.html (accessed 28 March 2022).

7 Stephen Emmott, *10 Billion* (Penguin, 2013), p 124.

8 https://www.bbc.com/future/bespoke/follow-the-food/why-soil-is-disappearing-from-farms/ (accessed 28 March 2022).

THE CLIMATE PENDULUM

When it comes to thinking about the environment as a Christian, there are two equal and opposite reactions to be aware of. The first reaction is the **panicked response**. This is where all things green become all that matters. It's the reaction that results in people gluing themselves to public buildings or blocking ambulances from travelling down the road. It's the urgent reaction modelled by scientists Dr Randall Mindy and Kate Dibiasky in the Netflix sensation *Don't Look Up*. Mindy and Dibiasky are so convinced of and worried about a pending global disaster (spoiler alert: a comet is due to hit earth and wipe out all life within six months—in the movie, I hasten to add) that they go on a giant media tour, desperate to wake the world up from its complacency.

Even if we're not about to jump on a tour bus, we might find ourselves feeling increasingly anxious, not to mention powerless, at the thought of an imminent climate-change tsunami. We're in make-or-break territory. Change or die. The very survival of the planet, indeed of all of humanity—especially the next generation, if not our own—is at stake. Something needs to be done, and it needs to be done now.

The other reaction is the **passive response**. When anything environmental gets raised, we simply shrug our shoulders or keep our head down maybe even roll our eyes—but basically we just carry on with life as it is. Life becomes like an in-real-time "green screen", where, just as with that fancy video-editing software, everything green mysteriously disappears. We might react this way for a number of reasons. Perhaps we've grown weary of all the alarmist rhetoric we see on the news, and so-called "climate-change fatigue" has caused us to mentally disengage from the topic. Or maybe we were never really engaged in the first place—we've got bigger problems to contend with. Or perhaps we've done our research and feel justified in our climate scepticism. After all, while it's almost undeniable that the climate is changing in some ways, the extent, the causes (specifically how much humans are to blame) and the solutions (how far the responsibility to reverse climate change lies with us) are far more contested. Maybe all this talk about climate change is just the latest "tree-hugging" fad.

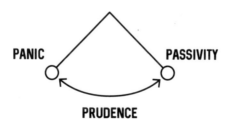

Or perhaps you find your inner climate pendulum swinging between both of these reactions, depending on what day of the week it is! Frankly, you don't know what to think from a Christian point of view when it comes to the environment—still less *what to do*.

I want to suggest a third reaction. The approach we'll take in this book is what we might call the **prudent response**. Here we'll try to avoid the extremes of panic and passivity by carefully digging into the topic from a whole-Bible perspective.

It must be said from the outset that Christians *can* and *will* legitimately disagree on many of the issues at play. We might land in different places on the exact causes of global warming, or on how to interpret the statistics, or on the role that governments should play in response, as well as on the many trade-offs that exist when it comes to formulating legislation (between, say, the cost of sustainable food production and the challenge of feeding a family on a low income). The cost of net zero is not cheap, but neither is the cost of doing nothing at all.

So, while we can debate the pros and cons of particular policies, the underlying principle of this book will be that, whether we lean to the left or to the right politically, Bible Christians need to take the environment seriously, in Bible ways.

And guess what? I believe that doing so is easier, and more important for the gospel, than you may think.

It's *easier* because the Christian worldview uniquely gives us the resources to engage prudently and purposefully in all things green. Unlike the atheist, we don't believe this physical world is all there is. We believe that God, who made our planet, owns it and rules it, and that he has promised "never again will I destroy all living creatures" (Genesis 8 v 21). We're not sitting on a ticking time bomb waiting for our world to explode. As we used to sing to our kids when they were little, "He's got the whole world in his hands". So we mustn't fall prey to panicked fixation. But neither must we passively sit by and ignore what's happening to God's world. We're stewards of his planet (Genesis 1 v 28; 2 v 15), and so not caring at all about deforestation, or plastic pollution, or global warming is not an option either. The Christian worldview uniquely enables us to avoid the extremes of panic and passivity.

Moreover, the fact that the environment is such a live issue in our culture gives us a wonderful and *important* opportunity to share that Christian worldview with others. For much of the time, holding a biblical position on a contemporary hot-button issue takes real conviction—and airing such a position in polite company takes great courage. For example, when conversations about sexuality or gender identity come up, it's extremely tempting to bury our heads in the sand, hoping the topic will change before too long. However, when it comes to the subject of the environment, I believe it's much easier to keep our heads up. Christian believers can cut along the grain of much contemporary discussion about green issues or climate change. This is God's world. Talking about the environment should feel like a home advantage.[9]

In fact, I have a sense that for Christians not to talk about the environment or play our part practically as best as we can might actually have a negative impact for the gospel. If Christians are seen as "mere talkers"—those who are happy to get you along to their church events but show no interest in, say, their use of single-use plastic or the sourcing of their coffee or the needs of the world in theirs prayers on a Sunday—that will undermine our gospel witness.

OBJECTION: "THE ONLY THING THAT MATTERS IS EVANGELISM"

"Sure, I'm happy to recycle and maybe even try to cycle to work a little more," you might be thinking. "But isn't it better to avoid getting caught up in all that other stuff? After all, the only thing that *really* matters is helping people get saved. All this talk about

---

9 This was precisely the experience of someone who shared with me that their getting involved in local environmental work in the community led to numerous gospel conversations.

climate change or carbon footprints or saving the planet is just a distraction, like playing the violin on the deck of the *Titanic*. Spiritual disaster is coming, and people just need to get into the lifeboat!"

Ever heard that kind of argument? Ever *made* that kind of argument? For me, it's "Yes" and "Yes"—because it's a compelling argument. People do need to be saved, and we do need to tell them how they can be saved. It's incredibly easy to be distracted from this vital task.

And yet there are a couple of problems with this "the only thing that matters is evangelism" argument. For one thing, no one *really* believes it. Or if they do, they don't live it. If the only thing that mattered was sharing the gospel, then we wouldn't (and shouldn't) do anything else! Like study at university or make sticky toffee pudding or comb our hair or read *The Gruffalo* to our kids or play chess, and so on. Now, some might say that the only reason you should do all those things is because ultimately they work towards sharing the gospel. ("I go to university to make non-Christian friends with whom I can share the gospel." Or "I make sticky toffee pudding to give to my sweet-toothed neighbour while I invite her to church". Or "I play chess so that I can use sacrificing my rook as an illustration of the gospel".) But in most of life we instinctively know that we're free to enjoy and engage with many aspects of the physical creation, and we don't think twice about it. Life would certainly be a lot less fun if we did.[10]

But more importantly, *the Bible* doesn't teach that "the only thing that matters is evangelism" either. Yes, the Bible is crystal clear on the need for people to be saved, and our responsibility to talk to people about Jesus so that they *can* be saved. To quote a neat though unattributed slogan, "Life is short, death is sure, sin the cause, Christ the cure". That message must shape our lives as believers and as churches. But the logical move from affirming these important convictions to saying that "the *only* thing that matters is evangelism" is not supported in Scripture. Even if evangelism is a top priority, that doesn't make everything else a non-priority.

There are lots of places in the Bible we could turn to see this. But let's consider just one.

There was a time, in ancient history, when disaster was coming, and people needed to get into the lifeboat. Quite literally. By which I mean the flood in Genesis 6 – 8, and Noah's famous ark.

WHY WAS THE ARK SO BIG?

Human sin was wreaking havoc. The world was a mess. So, God opened the heavens. But rather than

---

10 For more on this theme, see Julian Hardyman, *Maximum Life: Living Every Day of Your Life for Jesus* (IVP, 2011).

drowning all life on the earth, God intervened to bring about a rescue—because that's the kind of God he is. Noah, his wife, his three sons, and their three wives, were all kept safe in the ark. It was a wonderful act of salvation. And it points to the salvation that all humanity can find in Jesus. Get people into the lifeboat! Yes, and amen!

But what about all the animals?

If it's true that "the only thing that matters is evangelism" (implication: God is only really concerned about saving human beings from eternal judgment), then why does God tell Noah to make the ark so big? Why won't an eight-seater dinghy do? Why go to all the effort of making room for red pandas and Indian elephants and koalas? It is surely striking that at such a key, early point in salvation history—and in what is referred to in the New Testament as a paradigm of God's final judgment on the world (2 Peter 3 v 5-7)— the Lord is concerned about more than lost human beings. God genuinely has a heart for his world.[11]

---

11 Perhaps this conviction lies behind the tantalising last line of the book of Jonah, where the Lord states, "And should I not have concern for the great city of Nineveh, in which there are more than a hundred and twenty thousand people who cannot tell their right hand from their left—*and also many animals?*" (Jonah 4 v 11) (emphasis added).

WHAT TO EXPECT

Finally, you may be wondering what qualifies me to write an introduction to all things environmental. Let me give a few disclaimers. I'm not a specialist. I'm not a campaigner. I'm not a culture warrior. I'm not a lifelong Green voter! I'm simply a normal pastor with one foot in the Bible and one in the real world, longing to see how Scripture speaks to the big questions we face each day.

And it certainly has lots to say. Thinking Christianly about the environment will involve pulling together lots of important biblical categories, even in such a short book like this. During our study, we'll be dipping into the doctrines of creation (how things began in the first place), sin (what went wrong), humanity (what role we have), redemption (what the cross and resurrection of Jesus achieved), the end times (where it's all heading), and the mission of the church (what we should be about now). Some of the categories we'll get into are rather hotly contested, so we need to walk forward with humility and grace.

Is the Bible's message good news for our planet? Absolutely!

So let's start at the very beginning. Apparently, it's a very good place to start.

MY FATHER'S WORLD

CHAPTER 2

"Great are the works of the LORD, they are pondered by all who delight in them."

Psalm 111 v 2, inscribed in Latin over the entrance to the Cavendish Laboratory, home of the Department of Physics at the University of Cambridge, UK

Climate emergency. Microplastics. Megadrought. EV (electric vehicle). These are just a handful of new environment-related words added to the dictionary in 2022.[12] So what possible points of contact are there between the ancient words of the Bible and our modern conversations around COP27 or Extinction Rebellion or whether to buy an electric car? In this chapter we're going to begin to see that far from being an irrelevance to all things green, the

---

12 https://www.dictionary.com/e/new-dictionary-words-spring-2022/ (accessed 3 May 2022).

message of the Bible makes all the difference in the world. First up, creation.

WHAT A WONDERFUL WORLD

It all began so well. A perfect creator. A perfect creation. From great white sharks and kingfishers to Amazonian rainforests and wild raspberries—order was brought out of chaos; something came from nothing. In Genesis 1, in a breathtaking display of power, God speaks, and it is so. Behold cheetahs that can go from 0mph to 40mph in three strides.[13] Behold emperor penguins than can dive deeper than the height of the Empire State Building.[14] Behold more stars in the sky than human words that have ever been spoken.[15] If your instinctive reaction is "Woah!" then that is exactly the type of response that Genesis 1 invites us to give. The repeated refrain throughout the chapter is "God saw that it was good".

Creation, as God originally made it, was perfect in form and perfect in function, as evidenced by the fact that the trees in the Garden of Eden were both "pleasing to the eye and good for food"

---

13 https://www.thoughtco.com/how-fast-can-a-cheetah-run-4587031 (accessed 7 March 2022).

14 *The Week*, 24 August 2013 (accessed 7 March 2022).

15 http://blogs.scientificamerican.com/guest-blog/2013/10/08/10-sub-lime-wonders-of-science/ (accessed 7 March 2022).

(Genesis 2 v 9). Everything did what it was it was designed to do and did so perfectly. And why wouldn't it? Creation was the handiwork of the greatest designer of all.

It's worth acknowledging that the early chapters of Genesis have become a battleground for lots of Christians when it comes to piecing together the apparently conflicting claims of modern science and those of the Bible. We don't have the time or space in this short book to do justice to such a complex puzzle.[16] Suffice it to say that while the popular view is that science and religion are basically inversely proportional to each other (as one goes up, the other goes down), I'm convinced that science done well and the Bible studied well should lead to no contradiction at all.

But whatever our view on the *when* and *how* of creation, the focus in Genesis 1 – 2 is on who. God made it all, which means God owns it all: "The earth is the LORD's, and everything in it, the world, and all who live in it; *for he founded it on the seas and established it on the waters*" (Psalm 24 v 1-2, emphasis added). Planet Earth is God's intellectual property. Just as James Dyson owns the rights of his stunning cordless vacuum cleaner (it's revolutionised

---

16 Some good places to start are John Lennox, *Seven Days That Divide the World* (Zondervan, 2011) or Paul Garner, *The New Creationism: Building Scientific Theory on a Biblical Foundation* (Evangelical Press, 2009).

how we clean our house!), so God owns the rights to his stunning world. He writes the rules. Little wonder the Scriptures are replete with descriptions of creation testifying to the beauty of its Creator (see, for example, Psalm 19 v 1-6; Psalm 104; Romans 1 v 20).

All this is what theologians call the "doctrine of creation". Understood correctly, it should helpfully keep us on the straight and narrow as we think about the environment.

On the one hand, it should relieve us of the panicked response to environmental issues. The Great Barrier Reef or the Amazonian rainforest or the endangered Amur leopard might all be valuable and vulnerable things in God's world, but they are not *ultimate* things in God's world—because they are created things.

We need to beware overvaluing creation. The apostle Paul warned of the tendency to worship and serve "created things rather than the Creator" (Romans 1 v 25).[17] Have you ever considered that it is possible to make an idol of Planet Earth? When we do so, it both stifles our relationship with the Lord, robbing God of his glory, and can also overwhelm our wellbeing. When we invest all our hopes and

---

17 For more on this important biblical theme, see Timothy Keller, *Counterfeit Gods* (Hodder & Stoughton, 2010).

dreams and fears in something merely *created*—even something as important as the state of polar ice caps or topsoil quality or the need to clear plastic micro-fibres from our oceans—we put more pressure and expectations on "green solutions" than any created thing was designed to bear, which in turn can lead us into severe disillusionment.

On the other hand, the doctrine of creation should protect us from the passive disengagement that causes us to shrug our shoulders at all environmental concerns. I'm not to be laissez-faire about pollution or habitat destruction or the shrinking of the ozone layer; this is God's world. As I source and spend and steward the resources God has put at my disposal, I'm not to do so carelessly, selfishly tampering with the Creator's grand design. Why? Because this is God's world. Here's Francis Schaeffer:

> *If God treats the tree like a tree, the machine like a machine, the man like a man, shouldn't I as a fellow-creature, do the same ... And for the highest reason: because I love God—I love the One who has made it! Loving the Lover who has made it, I have respect for the thing He has made.*[18]

---

18 Francis Schaeffer, *Pollution and the Death of Man* (Tyndale House, 1973), p 57.

And so merely shrugging our shoulders at all things green isn't an option either. Such an approach may well avoid the ditch of making an idol of Planet Earth—but it might just make an idol of personal autonomy instead.

If God made this world and he owns it, then part of my Christian discipleship will mean putting in the hard yards of purposefully and prudently engaging with it, in ways that neither overvalue nor undervalue creation. As pastor and author Vaughan Roberts memorably puts it, "Matter matters because God made it".[19] And what God says goes.

THE SADDEST DAY

Only we humans decided to say, "No. Thanks for everything God, but you can leave now. We'd rather the gifts without the Giver. We'd rather make up our own rules instead of going with yours." Enter, stage left, sin—as the first man and woman eat from the one tree God has forbidden. And the New Testament makes it quite clear that if we'd have been there in the Garden of Eden, we'd have done just the same thing. And where there's sin, now death is round the corner too. Paul spells it out in Romans 5 v 12: "Sin entered the world through one man, and death through sin, and in this way death

---

19 Vaughan Roberts, *God's Big Picture* (IVP UK, 2002), p 28.

came to all people, because all sinned". Like father, like son. Every one of us is now born east of Eden with our backs turned to God—on death row.

The doctrine of sin assures us that sin gets everywhere. In fact, like a hideous, mutating virus, sin is so toxic and so virulent that its spread has affected more than just humanity. The entire natural world itself (and not just the humans within it) has been impacted by the fallout of the Fall. In Genesis 3 v 17, the Lord explains the consequence of man's disobedience that he will bring about on the natural world:

> *Cursed is the ground because of you; through painful toil you will eat food from it all the days of your life. It will produce thorns and thistles for you, and you will eat the plants of the field. By the sweat of your brow you will eat your food until you return to the ground, since from it you were taken; for dust you are and to dust you will return.*
>
> Genesis 3 v 17-19

Thorns, thistles and toil are now the order of the day. The apostle Paul's commentary on the same theme speaks of creation being "subjected to frustration" and in "bondage to decay", and "groaning as in the pains of childbirth right up to the present time" (Romans 8 v 20-23). It's as though a brick has been hurled against a glass window; cruel shards of death now radiate throughout creation. One of the interesting things about much of today's conversation around the environment is its distinctly moral tone: the damage being done to our planet is painted as a direct result of human ignorance, selfishness and greed. The implication is that if we could only stop being so selfish and learn how to work together, there might be hope for the world. And that's true—up to a point. The Bible agrees that, very often, bad behaviour reaps ill rewards—even in this life (for example, Proverbs 11 v 18). But it also goes further. The problem is not merely between humanity and planet. The root of the problem lies between humanity and God, which spills over to creation. Scripture's unique angle is that damage to the natural world is a consequence of human sin—an attitude towards our Creator which means that the whole creation is subjected to God's wrath as a result.

God is not ambivalent to such damage within his world. He doesn't just shrug his shoulders and move on to the humans. Instead, he reveals to the prophet Jeremiah his deep pain at the ruin of creation:

> *I will weep and wail for the mountains and take up a lament concerning the wilderness grasslands. They are desolate and untravelled, and the lowing of cattle is not heard. The birds have all fled and the animals are gone.*
>
> Jeremiah 9 v 10

Jeremiah asks God what has happened:

> *Who is wise enough to understand this? Who*
> *has been instructed by the LORD and can*
> *explain it? Why has the land been ruined and*
> *laid waste like a desert that no one can cross?*
>
> v 12

The LORD's reply:

> *It is because they have forsaken my law, which*
> *I set before them; they have not obeyed me or*
> *followed my law.* v 13

Granted, we need to be cautious about applying Old Testament prophecy to believers today. Jeremiah was writing at a time in salvation history when *the land* was central to the blessing of being God's people. Things are different this side of the coming of Christ. But, as Genesis 3 and Romans 8 made clear above, the Bible is clearly less shy about connecting the fate of the natural world with human behaviour than some of us tend to be.

THE RAINBOW AFTER THE RAIN

Wonderfully, none of this means that God is done with his world. Far from it. Indeed, straight after the flood, back in Genesis 8 and 9, the Lord makes a covenant with Noah, promising, "Never again will

I destroy all living creatures, as I have done. As long as the earth endures, seedtime and harvest, cold and heat, summer and winter, day and night will never cease" (Genesis 8 v 21-22). The rhythms of life on earth *will endure*. Season will follow season. Day will follow night.

This promise of God's round-the-clock protection of his world has no expiry date. God seals it with the rainbow and says, "Whenever the rainbow appears in the clouds, I will see it and remember the everlasting covenant between God and all living creatures of every kind on the earth" (9 v 14-16). The climate may well be changing, drastically even, but don't expect that to result in global extinction any time soon. God alone holds the destiny of this world in the palm of his hands, and for as long as he wants the earth to endure, it will. You can take his word for it.

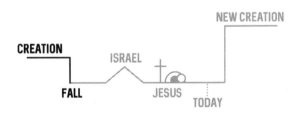

(Diagram not to scale!)

GETTING THE PENNY TO DROP

So does that mean we whack our central heating back up and turn all our lights on, before driving five minutes down the road to play Poohsticks with our single-issue plastics?! Erm, no. As we've seen, the doctrine of creation gives us pause for thought.

And yet it's still hard to rouse some of us into action (or even into decent reflection before action). I say that as someone who is still wiping sleep out of his eyes. This is God's world—fallen, yes, but still his. And it's dearly loved. So why are so many of us so passively ambivalent to the plight of God's creation?

This takes us back to our doctrine of sin. If we're honest, much of our disengagement can be less about principle and more about convenience. Often, we'd rather not think about it because we'd rather not do anything about it—especially if it might involve sacrifice on our part (for example, of time or money or convenience, and so on). We need to be aware of the reality that, as sinful and fallen people, we're often naturally inclined to choose the path of least resistance.

Or maybe we're choosing deliberately to zone out because we fear that just dipping in our toe might overwhelm us. We've seen the headlines, watched the documentaries, heard the activists and concluded, "What honest difference can we make?"

Short answer: if creation matters to God, it should matter to us. And in the words of Greta Thunberg's bestselling book, "No one is too small to make a difference". Just as it would be plain rude to turn my nose up at something one of my kids has made—even if it has got a little dog-eared—so it's plain rude to do the same to God's world. Love for God demands I take his creation seriously, even to take delight in what I see.

But it's more than that.

I have four kids. When I take an interest in one of their Lego models or drawings or wood carvings or pieces of modern calligraphy, each different creation reveals a different aspect of its creator. And the same is true with God. "The heavens declare the glory of God," wrote David in Psalm 19 v 1. Which means there are aspects of God's nature that—in his good providence—are expressed in the various songs that creation sings. The apostle Paul explained it this way:

> *For since the creation of the world God's invisible qualities—his eternal power and divine nature—have been clearly seen, being understood from what has been made, so that people are without excuse.* Romans 1 v 20

Why did God make galaxies and mountains and donkeys and trees? One answer is to teach us about himself.[20] For example, if lions became tragically extinct, and the Lord describes himself to us in lion-like terms (which he does, in Amos 1 v 2 or Revelation 5 v 5), then that vivid description of God's character (pointing to his ferocity at sin, or his mighty strength) will forever lose its power. Surely love for God must mean learning all we can about him from the world he's made. The same applies to learning from sparrows in Luke 12 v 6-7 (which reveal God's intimate knowledge of us) or from ravens in verse 24 (God's faithful provision). Put negatively, if aspects of God's self-revelation are brought to life for us through the world as it is now, then we've every reason to throw our energy behind trying to keep it that way.

There's a final evangelistic dimension, too, which we mustn't forget. The reality is that many of the real-world problems resulting from climate change, such as rising oceans, will have a direct impact on human beings. For example, as we saw in chapter 1, ten million Bangladeshis currently live below the "one-metre contour". The vast majority don't know Christ. Love for our neighbours demands that we sit up and take notice of their peril.

Why should Christians care about the environment? The Bible's answer, summarised in the

---

20 For one of the most mind-blowing books you'll ever read on this topic, check out Andrew Wilson, *God of All Things* (Zondervan, 2021).

doctrines of creation and sin, is *Because this world belongs to God*. We must neither overvalue nor undervalue it. And even this side of the fall, he cares deeply about our planet: both people and non-people.

If it matters to God, it should matter to us. And why wouldn't it? This is our Father's world. And we've got a vital role to play.

KINGS AND QUEENS OF NARNIA

CHAPTER 3

*What a piece of work is a man, How noble in
reason, how infinite in faculty, In form and
moving how express and admirable, In action
how like an Angel, In apprehension how like
a god, The beauty of the world, The paragon
of animals. And yet, to me, what is this
quintessence of dust?*

Hamlet 2.2, William Shakespeare

We have seen how the world has been created by
God but marred by sin, and how both realities
should have a huge bearing on our understanding
of the environment. We must neither overvalue the
world God has made nor undervalue it. Though
tragically fallen, creation still matters to God, and it
should matter to us too. But before moving on in the
Bible's story, we need to head back to the Garden of

Eden and look more closely at the pinnacle of God's creation: humans, including you and me!

The doctrine of humanity is important not just biblically but culturally. In much popular environmental rhetoric, the role of human beings in both the problem of climate change and its solution cannot be overstated. Here's the naturalist Sir David Attenborough—the most popular person in Britain, according to a 2021 YouGov survey[21]—in the climax to his BBC award-winning documentary *Planet Earth 2*:

> *We are at a unique stage in our history. Never before have we had such an awareness of what we are doing to the planet and never before have we had the power to do something about that. Surely, we have a responsibility to care for our blue planet. The future of humanity, and indeed all life on Earth, now depends on us.*[22]

"The future of ... all life on Earth ... depends on us." Responsibility doesn't come much bigger than that! Let's see if the Bible agrees.

---

21 https://yougov.co.uk/ratings/entertainment/popularity/people/all (accessed 20 January 2022).

22 *Planet Earth 2*, Episode 6 (BBC Studios).

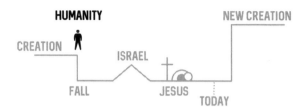

God's creation of humanity is described in both Genesis 1 and 2. Genesis 1 gives us the wide-angle-lens view, the 50,000-foot perspective. It describes the six days of creation, from planets to protons and everything in between. And the great climax—the *pièce de résistance*—occurs on day 6, with God's creation of humanity. Human beings are not merely the product of time plus matter plus chance. Humanity is where God's week of creation was heading all along: the purposeful, planned, perfect design of man and woman. Having evaluated each day of creation with the repeated refrain "God saw that it was good" (Genesis 1 v 10, 12, 18, 21, 25), at the end of day 6, the writer of Genesis tells us that "God saw all that he had made, and it was very good" (v 31).

Genesis 2 describes the same the event with a narrow-angle lens, from the ground up.

> *Now no shrub had yet appeared on the earth*
> *and no plant had yet sprung up, for the LORD*

> *God had not sent rain on the earth and there*
> *was no one to work the ground, but streams*
> *came up from the earth and watered the whole*
> *surface of the ground. Then the LORD God*
> *formed a man from the dust of the ground and*
> *breathed into his nostrils the breath of life,*
> *and the man became a living being.*
>
> Genesis 2 v 5-7

Notice the incredible tenderness—Adam is intricately moulded together, like a lifesize clay model. He's brought to life with divine breath.

And the creation of Eve is no less intimate:

> *But for Adam no suitable helper was found.*
> *So the LORD God caused the man to fall into a*
> *deep sleep; and while he was sleeping, he took*
> *one of the man's ribs and then closed up the*
> *place with flesh. Then the LORD God made a*
> *woman from the rib he had taken out of the*
> *man, and he brought her to the man.*
>
> Genesis 2 v 20-22

If Genesis 1 shows God's great power, Genesis 2 shows his great precision. Think about a boss at work. It takes great power for him to be able to say "Coffee!" and minutes later a coffee appears (courtesy of a helpful intern). But for the boss to go into the staff room, where there's a posh coffee machine, and personally grind the beans and foam the milk and pour the espresso and hand-craft a flat white… That takes great precision.

There's nothing slapdash about God's creation—he didn't just bang it out. Nor is God aloof from his creation—he didn't merely hide away in his heavenly home, firing out orders at will. His design of Adam and Eve in Genesis 2 is utterly, gloriously meticulous and tender. Human beings are truly "fearfully and wonderfully made" (Psalm 139 v 14).

IN A LEAGUE OF THEIR OWN

It's important that we hold these two creation accounts together. Read as a whole, its clear from Genesis 1 – 2 that human beings are very much part of creation. Humans were made on day 6, along with the animals. They're made by God's word, just like everything else. *Dust we are, and to dust we will return* (3 v 19). There's an evident similarity between us and the world around us. We're all made up of the same building blocks—atoms of hydrogen, oxygen, carbon, nitrogen and so on, all doing their thing.

But there's a clear *difference* too. Human beings are unmistakably set apart from the rest of creation. We've already seen God's unique verdict of "very good" after his creation of humanity in

Genesis 1 v 31. Indeed, God uniquely announces, "Let us make mankind" as he brings the first humans to life (v 26—"us" being an early hint perhaps of God's triune nature) as opposed to "Let there be..." which is how he makes everything else. And of course, it's only Adam (shortly followed by Eve) who gets the full hand-crafted, divine breath-of-life treatment (2 v 7 and 21-22). But surely the clearest sign of mankind's difference is seen in God's declaration in Genesis 1 v 26-27. Human beings are uniquely made in *the image of God*:

> *Then God said, "Let us make mankind in our*
> *image, in our likeness, so that they may rule*
> *over the fish in the sea and the birds in the sky,*
> *over the livestock and all the wild animals,*
> *and over all the creatures that move along the*
> *ground." So God created mankind in his own*
> *image, in the image of God he created them;*
> *male and female he created them.*   v 26-27

Whole ink pots have been spilled trying to explain what it means to be made in God's image. Vaughan Roberts gives a helpful summary: we were created to reflect God (for example, in our rationality, morality, sociability and creativity), represent God (by lovingly ruling creation), and relate to God (to know and be known by our heavenly Father.[23] And while the fall has changed much about God's world, the Bible makes it clear that humanity's in-God's-image-ness continues.[24]

In the C.S. Lewis novel *Prince Caspian*, Trufflehunter the badger reflects on the damage that has taken place in Narnia in the years since its human rulers—Peter, Susan, Edmund and Lucy—left. Trufflehunter is explaining to two sceptical dwarfs, Nikabrik and Trumpkin, how incredible it is to have found Prince Caspian—another human being—in the woods…

> *"This is the true King of Narnia. And we beasts remember, even if Dwarfs forget, that Narnia was never right except when a Son of Adam was King."*
>
> *"Whistles and whirligigs, Trufflehunter!" said Trumpkin. "You don't mean you want to give the country to Humans?"*
>
> *"I said nothing about that," answered the Badger. "It's not Men's country (who should*

---

23 See Vaughan Roberts, *God's Big Design* (IVP, 2005), p 39-42.

24 For instance, in Genesis 9 v 3 God gives humans permission to eat meat, and not just vegetables, which constituted the pre-fall diet in Genesis 1 v 29. So it isn't a sin to take the life of an animal—but God underlines that it is a sin to shed the blood of a fellow human, "for in the image of God has God made mankind" (Genesis 9 v 6).

know that better than me?) but it's a country
for a man to be King of. We Badgers have long
enough memories to know that. Why, bless us
all, wasn't the High King Peter a Man?"[25]

What is true of Narnia is true of our world: "It's not
Men's country … but it's a country for a man to
be King of" (with, we might add, a woman). This
is our Father's world. It's not our country. But in
our Father's good and wise design, it's a world he
wants us to be kings and queens of. We're to rule
over creation, under God's rule. We're to "be fruitful
and increase in number, fill the earth and subdue it"
(Genesis 1 v 28).

But what exactly does that look like on the
ground? And how do we avoid the slide from biblical
dominion into unbiblical domination?

I, HUMAN, TAKE YOU, PLANET EARTH

To answer those questions, we're going to start by
pulling out a Hebrew dictionary. The Hebrew text
of the Old Testament has lots of clever word-plays
that are easy to miss in our English translations.[26]
In Genesis 2 v 7, God forms the man (in Hebrew,

---

25 C.S. Lewis, *Prince Caspian* (Lion, 1980), p 64.

26 I am indebted to David Hegeman, *Plowing in Hope: Toward a Biblical Theology of Culture* (Canon Press, 2004), p 42-44, for this stimulating insight.

"adam") from dust of the ground (*adam-ah*). While chronologically, it was the ground that came first, linguistically, the *adamah* is taken from the root word "adam". Then in verse 23, at the creation of Eve, Adam calls her "woman" (*ish-shar*) because she was taken out of man (and here, interestingly, the Hebrew uses a different word for man: *ish*).

man // ground
adam // adam-ah

husband // wife
ish // ish-shar

A helpful analogy may be drawn here. Theologian David Hegeman explains:

> *Just as the ish is the husband of the ishshah (wife), so the man (adam) is the husband of the ground (adamah). As a husband is expected to lovingly provide for his bride, cherishing and nourishing her (Ephesians 5 v 29), and thereby enhancing her health and beauty, so the man was to work and keep the ground/ earth, enhancing its fruitfulness. Likewise, just as a husband will gain children only if he "interacts" with his wife, so the earth will yield its fruit only through "culturative interaction".*

The English language ironically captures this idea with the word husbandry.[27]

So, as Hegeman goes on to explain, our human calling is to avoid both *withdrawing from creation*—which is the temptation of those of us who lean towards panic (where we're nervous about the lasting imprint of humanity on the planet)—and *abusing creation*—which is the temptation of those who tend towards passivity (where we're quick to turn a blind eye to the ecological consequences of human activity). Only then will we be free to lovingly *rule creation*, as we "preserve and develop the earth's hidden potential and fruitfulness" in life-giving, environmentally sustainable ways.[28]

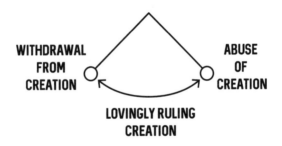

WITHDRAWAL FROM CREATION

ABUSE OF CREATION

LOVINGLY RULING CREATION

---

27 Hegeman, *Plowing in Hope*, p 43.

28 As above.

SNAPSHOTS FROM THE OLD TESTAMENT

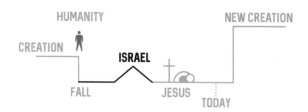

God has always wanted his people to exercise dominion, not domination, over the world around them. Moving forward through the Bible's timeline, in the Old Testament law we find some wonderful insights into how the people of Israel were to rule creation sustainably—forgoing short-term gain in favour of long-term fruitfulness. Here's one example:

> *If you come across a bird's nest beside the road, either in a tree or on the ground, and the mother is sitting on the young or on the eggs, do not take the mother with the young. You may take the young, but be sure to let the mother go, so that it may go well with you, and you may have a long life.*
>
> Deuteronomy 22 v 6-7

It's easy to see the logic. If you take the young and leave the mother, then you'll get more birds soon enough. But if you take the young and the mother, then before long you'll have no more birds at all. So, if creation is going to be sustained, mother birds need to get a free pass.

Or here's another example, this time talking about deforestation in the context of warfare:

> *When you lay siege to a city for a long time,*
> *fighting against it to capture it, do not destroy*
> *its trees by putting an axe to them, because you*
> *can eat their fruit. Do not cut them down. Are*
> *the trees people, that you should besiege them?*
> *However, you may cut down trees that you*
> *know are not fruit trees and use them to build*
> *siege works until the city at war with you falls.*
> Deuteronomy 20 v 19-20

Next time you're capturing a city, make sure you leave the fruit trees behind. Why? Because, as well as the obvious pragmatic point about fruit trees producing fruit to eat (doh), the law hints at something more profound: *What did trees ever to do you?* "Are the trees people, that you should besiege them?" The Israelites are permitted to use the trees for their appropriate purposes (food or wood, depending on the type)— but wanton destruction of other living things just for the sake of it is plain wrong.

This goes to illustrate that we shouldn't feel guilty about using the world's natural resources; it's why God put them there. But there are bad ways of doing so—ways that go way beyond what is healthy and loving and sustainable. Israel was to rule creation, yes, but with love and respect.

The principle of ruling creation with love for God and neighbour was also seen in Israel's agriculture laws. One year in every seven, the Israelites were to give the land a breather—a Sabbath rest—when there was to be no sowing or reaping or pruning (Leviticus 25 v 2-7). Then, once every "7 x 7" years, in the 50th year, there was to be a year of Jubilee (v 8-17), when, as well as receiving its regulation Sabbath rest, the land was to be reallocated around the people, ensuring that everyone was provided for.[29] Moreover, the later wisdom literature concurs: "The righteous care for the needs of their animals, but the kindest acts of the wicked are cruel" (Proverbs 12 v 10).[30] Both people and planet are important.

JESUS: A SECOND ADAM

Of course, this was all the *ideal*—the divine instruction manual, as it were. Sadly, the history of Israel shows that God's people constantly failed to keep it,

---

29 Douglas J. Moo and Jonathan A. Moo, *Creation Care: A Biblical Theology of the Natural World* (Zondervan, 2018), p 88-97.

30 Thus the Premier League footballer who does keepy-uppies with his cat will only find strong condemnation from the pages of Scripture. https://www.theguardian.com/football/2022/feb/09/kurt-zouma-cat-backlash-calls-for-prosecution-west-ham (accessed 7 March 2022). It especially pains me to share this story as a West Ham fan.

despite his constant grace. Mercifully, of course, this was not the end of the story. Enter the carpenter.

Nothing affirms the significance of the physical creation more than the incarnation of Jesus. We might expect God to be above getting his hands dirty. And yet the Creator became part of the creation. Jesus is the perfect "image of the invisible God" (Colossians 1 v 15). "The Word became flesh" (John 1 v 14). "God is spirit" (4 v 24)—but he became physical. He entered our environment.

But the "creatureliness" of Jesus didn't finish with his incarnation. It's fascinating to observe how embedded Jesus' whole life and ministry was in the physical world. He was the adopted son of a carpenter (Matthew 13 v 55). He used flowers and birds to teach his followers not to worry but trust in God's lavish provision (Matthew 6 v 25-34). He used a fig tree to warn people of the fruitlessness of empty religion (Mark 11 v 12-14, 20-21). He used a popular was of predicting the weather (the 1st-century equivalent to "Red sky at night, shepherd's delight") to warn the Jewish leaders against unbelief (Matthew 16 v 1-4). He ate, drank, slept, wept, spat, sailed, slept and sat down (Matthew 9 v 10; John 4 v 7; 11 v 35; Mark 7 v 33; 4 v 38; Matthew 5 v 1). He rode a donkey (Mark 11 v 7). And then he died on a physical cross (John 19 v 18). He was buried in a physical tomb (v 41-42). On the morning of his resurrection, he was even mistaken for the gardener (20 v 15).

At every turn, the goodness and importance of creation is reiterated. To quote the Legend of Gondor from *The Lord of the Rings*, "The hands of the king are the hands of a healer, and so shall the rightful king be known".[31]

It's little wonder that the apostle Paul describes Jesus as a second Adam (Romans 5 v 12-19), who did what the first Adam failed to do. Here's how American pastor Tim Keller explains it:

> *At the beginning of history there was also a garden and a command. God put Adam and Eve in that garden, and they were told not to eat of the Tree. The direction was: "Obey me about the Tree, and you will live"—obey me and I'll bless you. But they disobeyed. Now there is another garden, and a Second Adam, and another command. Jesus Christ has been sent by the Father to go to the cross, which is also a tree. To the first Adam he said, "Obey me about the Tree and I will bless you"—and Adam didn't do it. But to the second Adam he says, "Obey me about the Tree [meaning the cross] and I will crush you"—and Jesus does.*[32]

31 J. R. R. Tolkein, *The Return of the King* (Del Ray, 2012), p 138.
32 Timothy Keller, *Encounters with Jesus* (Hodder, 2013), p 163.

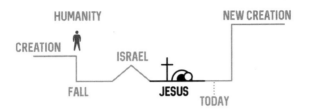

Where Adam failed, Christ prevailed. And having taken our sin and shame and death on himself as he died, three days later Jesus rose again, offering forgiveness and freedom and life to all who call on his name, which means there's grace to cover our failures, including those relating to our care of the environment. The numerous ways in which we've fallen short of lovingly ruling God's world can be left in the grave—instead, we can look to the future having been renewed in our service of him.

ONE SAVIOUR

There is one Saviour of the world. And it's not you or me.

We began this chapter with Sir David Attenborough, from *Planet Earth 2*. Let's revisit his words:

> *We are at a unique stage in our history. Never before have we had such an awareness of what we are doing to the planet [agreed] and never before have we had the power to do something*

about that [agreed]. Surely, we have a respon-
sibility to care for our blue planet [agreed].
The future of humanity, and indeed all life on
Earth, now depends on us [not so much].

Our study of Scripture would agree with much of
Sir David's analysis. But it's his last line that sticks
in the throat. Saying that "the future of humanity,
indeed all life on Earth, now depends on us" is
simply too crushing for us to bear. I prefer the con-
clusion of former Dutch prime minister and theologian Abraham Kuyper: "There is not a square inch
in the whole domain of human existence over which
Christ, who is Sovereign, does not cry, 'Mine!'"[33]

The biblical doctrine of humanity guards us
against both the panicked response that suggests it's
within our power to save the planet (it isn't) and the
passivity that means we prefer to shirk all responsibility for anything green (we mustn't). Instead,
we're to serve Christ faithfully wherever he's placed
us. Human beings have been made in God's image
to rule over creation, under God's rule. The planet
might be our Father's world by right, but it's been
given to us as his stewards. "The highest heavens

---

33 Kuyper's famous quote was given at his inaugural lecture at the open-
ing of the Free University in 1880. See James D. Bratt, ed., *Abraham*
Kuyper: A Centennial Reader (Eerdmans, 1998), p.488. Many thanks
to Michael Baldwin for helping me chase down the reference!

belong to the LORD, *but the earth he has given to the human race*" (Psalm 115 v 16, emphasis added). And so, we roll up our sleeves in our studies or our science or our stewardship of his world.[34] But we go to sleep at night trusting the Lord Jesus to be the Saviour of the world. We don't have to carry the weight of the world on our shoulders—that job's already taken.

---

34 See the helpful resources by London Institute for Contemporary Christianity.

TOMORROW NEVER DIES

CHAPTER FOUR

*"Gandalf! I thought you were dead! But then I
thought I was dead myself.
Is everything sad going to come untrue? What's
happened to the world?"
"A great Shadow has departed," said Gandalf,
and then he laughed and the sound was like
music, or like water in a parched land; and
as he listened the thought came to Sam that
he had not heard laughter, the pure sound of
merriment, for days upon days without count."*

The Return of the King, J. R. R. Tolkein

Moving home is one of life's big events. Before
our last big move, my wife spent months sort-
ing and shifting, boxing or binning the vast amounts
of stuff that we had accrued over the years. If you've
ever moved house, you'll know that in the run-up,

the things around you start to look a little different: the paint peeling off the bathroom wall, the smell of damp in the spare room, the garden that's got out of control. Where previously they got you down or were jobs on the to-do list that never quite got done, well now—with the removal van on its way—you suddenly find you can make do because soon this won't be your home and those things won't be your problem. You're moving on.

We've been seeing how the Bible urges us to take the environment seriously, avoiding the extremes of panic and passivity. Most of our time has been spent near the *start* of the Bible's story. Now we're going to fast forward to the end. What bearing do the Bible's promises about the future have on our approach to all things green today?

HOME SWEET HOME

But first, a very small question, with a very big answer. *Is this world your home?*

On the one hand, there's the simple case for saying *no*. If you're a Christian, this world is not your home, and nor is it mine. Despite the pull of life in the here and now, "our citizenship is in heaven" (Philippians 3 v 20). The apostle Paul reminds the Corinthians that walking by faith and not by sight means preferring "to be away from the body and at home with the Lord" (2 Corinthians 5 v 7-8). Peter seems to agree, describing his readers as "foreigners and exiles" (1 Peter 2 v 11) and clearly playing on the Old Testament language of exile—away from home. And Jesus himself spoke famous words of comfort to his disciples in the upper room:

> *My Father's house has many rooms; if that were not so, would I have told you that I am going there to prepare a place for you? And if I go and prepare a place for you, I will come back and take you to be with me that you also may be where I am.*　　　John 14 v 2-3

Putting all this together, the implication definitely seems to be that one day we'll move out of this place (that is, our earthly bodies and this fallen world), and go to another place—a better place. The removal van is on its way, and we're off to a new home: heaven.

So is *heaven* our home? In one sense, yes. But on the other hand, the situation is a little bit more complicated than that. For starters, we need to think more about that word "heaven".

WHAT ON EARTH IS HEAVEN?[35]

If popular culture is to be believed, heaven is a place of white-nightie-wearing, harp-playing floatiness, where everyone goes around with a very faint glow. More recently, TV programmes like *The Good Place* suggest that heaven is where everyone's wishes come true, whenever they want, so long as they've been good enough to get there.

However, when we open our Bibles, a rather different picture emerges. Here the word "heaven" is used in several different ways. It's sometimes used meteorologically to describe the sky above, as opposed to the earth beneath.[36] It can also refer to what we might call "divine space", where God lives, in contrast to the "physical space" of Planet Earth.[37]

What Christians often think of as "heaven"—that is, the ultimate glorious future destiny of all who've turned from sin and trusted in Jesus (as opposed to the painful alternative of hell for all who haven't)—the Bible refers to as "the new heavens and the new earth" (Revelation 21 v 1). We often shorten this to "the new creation".

---

35 I've shamelessly stolen this question from the title of James Paul's excellent book *What on Earth Is Heaven?* (IVP UK, 2021).

36 For example, Genesis 1 v 1, "In the beginning God created the heavens and the earth" (Genesis 1 v 1) or Psalm 19 v 1, "The heavens declare the glory of God; the skies proclaim the work of his hands".

37 Twenty-three times in the Bible, God is referred to as "the God of heaven". Elsewhere the Lord announces through the prophet Isaiah, "Heaven is my throne, and the earth is my footstool" (Isaiah 66 v 1).

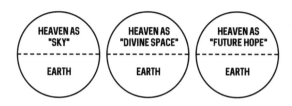

It's absolutely true that when we die, if we're trusting in Jesus, we go to be with him. To be "away from the body" is to be "at home with the Lord" (2 Corinthians 5 v 8). There is life after death "in heaven", so to speak. But the ultimate hope for the believer is what former Bishop of Durham Tom Wright memorably calls "Life after life after death"—the future, embodied existence of all God's people, gloriously risen again in a "new creation", after the return of King Jesus:[38]

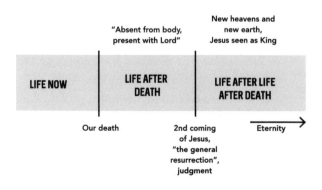

---

38 See Tom Wright, *Surprised by Hope* (SPCK, 2007).

While it's common for people to comfort themselves with the idea that loved ones are "up in heaven" or "looking down on us", the theologian Ian K. Smith argues that "the Bible is more concerned about God coming down to earth than humans going up to heaven". We see such a "downward movement in Eden, the tabernacle, in the temple, in the incarnation, in the resurrection, and in the second coming".[39] Time and again in the Bible, God comes "down" to meet us here—and he will do so again. Paul describes the second coming of Jesus in this way:

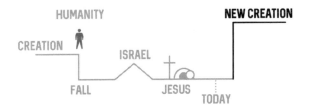

We believe that Jesus died and rose again, and so we believe that God will bring with Jesus those who have fallen asleep in him ... **The Lord himself will come down from heaven, with a loud command, with the voice of the archangel and with the trumpet call of God, and the dead in Christ will rise first.** *After*

39 Ian K. Smith, *Not Home Yet: How God's Renewal of the Earth Fits into God's Plan for the World* (Crossway, 2019), p 13.

> *that, we who are still alive and are left will*
> *be caught up together with them in the clouds*
> *to meet the Lord in the air. And so we will be*
> *with the Lord forever.*
>
> 1 Thessalonians 4 v 14, 16 (emphasis added)

The language of *meeting the Lord in the air* has been understood by some as the grand departure (or "rapture") of Christians from Planet Earth, before being whisked away to eternal pastures new.[40] However, I'm convinced that Paul is instead describing a grand "welcoming home" party as expectant believers usher the Lord Jesus back to earth.[41] This is the return of the King! In fact, Paul's encouragement of believers in Philippians 3 with the truth that "our citizenship is in heaven" (v 20) concludes similarly: "And we eagerly await a Saviour from there, the Lord Jesus Christ, who, by the power that enables him to bring everything under his control, will transform our lowly bodies so that they will be like his glorious body" (v 20-21).

Here's Ian K. Smith again:

> *Jesus's return to earth is the focus of the Christian's hope, and this return will not just be for a visit, to pick us up and take us home to heaven.*

---

40 For example, in the popular *Left Behind* series of books and movies by Tim LaHaye and Jerry B. Jenkins.

41 Gene L. Green, *1 Thessalonians* (Apollos, 2002), p 226.

He is coming to stay. The new Jerusalem will descend to earth, and we will be at home, with Jesus, on earth.[42]

And this isn't just good news for us, but for the whole planet: "For the creation was subjected to frustration, not by its own choice, but by the will of the one who subjected it, in hope that *the creation itself will be liberated from its bondage to decay and brought into the freedom and glory of the children of God*" (Romans 8 v 19-22, emphasis added). The return of the king will mean the renewal and restoration of his world.

LIVING WITH THE END IN VIEW

So back to our initial question: *is this world your home?* We've seen the case for a simple "no". For the Christian believer, home is away from life in the here and now, and with the Lord for ever. Why bother too much about the peeling paint or the smell of damp—or, indeed, the plummeting biodiversity and widespread deforestation? The removal van is on its way.

But now we've seen that there's more to the future of this world than we might have first thought. And

---

42 Ian K. Smith, *Not Home Yet*, p 13-14. See also Jim Paul, *What on Earth Is Heaven?* (IVP UK, 2021).

being clear on that future will give us a vital perspective when it comes to engaging with the environment. Four particular areas come into focus.

1. Accountability

When Jesus comes back "to judge the living and the dead" (in the words of the Apostles' Creed), we'll have to give an account to God for how we've lived our lives: every word said (or not said), every deed done (or not done), even our thoughts and our motives. It will all be under Jesus' spotlight. In the parable of the minas in Luke 19 v 11-27, ten servants are entrusted with their master's money in his absence and held accountable for what they have done with it upon his return. The parable picks up this theme of accountability and focuses on *stewardship*. What are we doing with what we've been given while the master's away?

There are a number of valid applications here, such as how well we've stewarded our spiritual gifts, or the opportunities before us, or the resources at our disposal, or even the amount of knowledge we've had of God and his ways. As Jesus explained elsewhere, "From everyone who has been given much, much will be demanded" (Luke 12 v 48).

But for the purposes of this book, surely our stewardship of the planet bears reflecting on. It's as if

Jesus has said to us, *Here, have a planet to look after. Made specially by me. Let's see what you can do with it. I'm going away for a while, but I look forward to seeing the results!*

Those of us who lean more towards passivity on matters of the environment may find ourselves looking frighteningly like the guy who shrugged his shoulders of all responsibility and decided to bury his mina in the ground.

The principle: We'll answer to Jesus about how we used his world. Being careless with something that wasn't ours in the first place won't go down well.

2. Witness

When Jesus returns, *everyone* will have to give an account before him—that includes our unbelieving family and friends, as well as people who've never heard his name. This means that we need to do all we can in order not just to be ready to meet Jesus ourselves but to help others do the same.

Perhaps those of us who lean more towards the panicked response, where all things green are the only things that matter, need to be especially careful here. It's not impossible for our understandable concern about the planet to squeeze out concern for the *actual people* who live here. To put it in the starkest terms, yes, failing soil quality and melting polar ice caps are a huge global worry with enormous consequences, both now and in the future. But neither the land nor the sea needs to repent and believe before Jesus returns. Countless people still need to get to the lifeboats before it's too late. One day it will be.

The principle: Don't allow creation care to force personal evangelism down the agenda. Sharing the hope of the gospel must always be high priority for Christians, given the Lord's return.

3. Timescales

Much of the climate literature you read is extraordinarily apocalyptic. Remember Greta Thunberg in our introduction: "I want you to panic. I want you to act as if your house was on fire. Because it is." Greta sees herself as sounding the earth's fire alarm, because nothing less than a blaring siren will move us into the action necessary to avert the pending disaster.

Granted, some of the more vocal campaigners haven't got the best track record when it comes to pinning down their timings. Back in 2009, for example, former US Vice President Al Gore infamously predicted that "there is a 75% chance that the entire north polar ice cap, during some of the summer months, could be completely ice-free within the next five to seven years". Yes, the ice caps are continuing to melt, but "completely ice-free" by 2016 was some way off the mark.

More importantly, from a biblical perspective the future is quite clear. The most important remaining date on the world's calendar and the last great job on the Lord Jesus' to-do list is for him to return in glory and power. That might happen before you finish this book. It might happen next year. It might even be scores of millennia away, such that the 2020s will end up being considered part of the early church! No one knows when Jesus will return—only the Father (Mark 13 v 32-37).

And until he does, the world *will carry on*. Remember God's covenant with creation after the flood: "As long as the earth endures, seedtime and harvest, cold and heat, summer and winter, day and night will never cease" (Genesis 8 v 22). *Life* will carry on. When Jesus returns, he won't be coming back to a dystopian wasteland, an empty shell of what once was. People will be alive and will be waiting to welcome his arrival (1 Thessalonians 4 v 15-17).

The principle: As threatening as the climate crisis may be, human life on earth will not end before Jesus comes back. And God alone is privy to the timescales.

4. Continuity

When the Lord Jesus returns, he's not going to head to some other world. He's coming back here: this earth—purified, refined, made new.

Throughout 1 Corinthians 15, Paul is at pains to draw a parallel between what happened to Jesus (death and resurrection at the first Easter) and what will happen to his people (death and resurrection when Christ returns). It is striking to observe that while there was definitely *discontinuity* between that first Good Friday and Easter Day (the risen Jesus could appear and disappear, for instance), there was also clear *continuity* too. The same Jesus who went into tomb came out three days later. He invited Thomas to feel his scars. He wasn't consumed or annihilated or switched for a later model; he was resurrected, changed, renewed. Or, as Paul puts it, "Sown in dishonour ... raised in glory ... sown a natural body ... raised a spiritual body" (1 Corinthians15 v 43-44). The story of Jesus will be story of his world: resurrection. This planet, changed and renewed.[43]

---

43 On the surface, 2 Peter 3 v 10-13 appears to imply the opposite. For example, "The heavens will disappear with a roar; the elements will be destroyed by fire" (v 10). However, scratch beneath the surface and a slightly different picture begins to emerge. For one thing, the word "element" here is actually the New Testament word for the "elemental" or fundamental powers of this sinful world. This is less about zapping atoms of carbon and oxygen, and more about the destruction of everything and everyone that stands against God. (See

All of which makes it clear that despite our best attempts at messing God's world up, he's not written it off. There's life in the old planet yet! In one of the most majestic passages in all of Scripture on the supremacy of Christ, Paul explains: "For God was pleased to have all his fullness dwell in him, and *through him to reconcile to himself all things*, whether things on earth or things in heaven, by making peace through his blood, shed on the cross" (Colossians 1 v 19-20, emphasis added). There is no fudging the clear cosmic dimensions to our salvation. Whatever this means (and it's hard to pin down exactly), it would seem to be more than just getting people into lifeboats.

And so, rather than clock-watching for the removal van, with our eyes fixed on getting out of here as soon as we can, the prudent response will mean rolling our sleeves up with creation-affirming activities (for example, animal conservation or renewable energy research or reducing waste) that cut with the grain of the God who's not planning on writing off the planet anytime soon. Or ever. When we serve the God of resurrection, no labour for the Lord is ever in vain (1 Corinthians 15 v 58).

Dave Bookless, *Planetwise: Dare to Care for God's World* (IVP UK, 2008), p 83-84.) What's more, in verses 5-7 Peter talks of the earth being "destroyed" by the flood. This was certainly a devastating act of cosmic judgment (see Genesis 6)—yet even then, the earth was not annihilated but refined and purified by God's judgment. The same will be true of the judgment Jesus brings upon his return.

The principle: The fact that Jesus will one day restore and renew his world gives greater significance to any beautifying creational acts we do while we wait.

THE DIVINE REPAIR SHOP

One of our family's favourite TV programmes is *The Repair Shop*. The format is pretty simple: the presenter, Jay Blades, and a team of master craftspeople turn beloved family heirlooms—worn down and warped and cracked and chipped and rusted and threadbare—into things of exquisite beauty.

Imagine you went on *The Repair Shop* with a beloved, dishevelled, moth-eaten teddy bear. You hand it over to Jay, and his team sets to work. You return two days later for the big reveal, only for a brand new teddy bear to be presented to you. "That's lovely," you say, "but where's my bear?" "Oh, we replaced it," explains Jay. "You replaced it?! I don't want a replacement bear. I want my bear. I thought my bear was going to be restored and renewed!"

Or imagine you apply to take a toy go-kart in. It's been lovingly played with by the family for generations. To say it's seen better days is an understatement—it's seen better decades. The pedal mechanism has completely rusted, bits of leather are peeling off the seat and the metal trim around the door is bent out of shape. If people didn't know otherwise, they'd see it in your garage and assume it was heading straight for the scrap heap, and so who cares how you treat it? Why *wouldn't* you just pick all the leather away, or smash it into a tree, or leave it outside in the rain?

But you don't do that—because you know it's got a bright future ahead of it. It's got a date with *The Repair Shop*, where it's going to be wonderfully restored and renewed and made better than ever. And knowing that that future is on the cards, far from making you more slapdash and laissez-faire in your use of the go-kart, instead makes you want to take even *more* care of it. There's life in the old go-kart yet! So, you look after it and enjoy using it and do your best to preserve it, and all the while, you look forward to the day when Jay Blade and his incredible team work their resurrection magic on it once and for all.

If what the craftspeople on *The Repair Shop* can do is cool, just imagine what the Lord Jesus will make with the raw ingredients of Planet Earth when he returns. It makes the spine tingle just thinking about it. And it should move us to take care of what he's given us, for his praise and glory.

Little wonder the psalmist bursts into song in anticipation of all the Lord will do on his return:

Let the heavens rejoice, let the earth be glad;
let the sea resound, and all that is in it.
Let the fields be jubilant, and everything in
them;
let all the trees of the forest sing for joy.
Let all creation rejoice before the LORD, for he
comes,
he comes to judge the earth.
He will judge the world in righteousness
and the peoples in his faithfulness.

Psalm 96 v 11-13

NO ONE IS TOO SMALL TO MAKE A DIFFERENCE

POSTSCRIPT[44]

We're nearly at the end of our study of the Bible's view of the environment. Most of our time has been spent trying to connect the Bible's timeless truths to our contemporary concerns for the planet. We've sought to avoid the extremes of panic and passivity by making the case for prudent engagement in all things green. However, one danger of such an introductory book as this is that we can end up thinking, "Ok, I'm persuaded that I need to engage with environmental concerns. I'm not going to obsess over them, but I don't want to be ambivalent. I want to do something. But what now?"

---

44 This title has been taken from the best-selling book by Greta Thunberg, *No One Is Too Small to Make a Difference* (Penguin, 2019).

It's a good question to ask if we're going to avoid being like those who look in the mirror and immediately forget what they look like (James 1 v 23-24). We need to heed the words of James: "Do not merely listen to the word, and so deceive yourselves. Do what it says" (James 1 v 22).

So here, with the hope of inspiring you, is a day-in-the-life account of what it might look like to engage prudently as a Christian with environmental concerns. The solutions to the issues facing our planet are complex, and the realistic choices available to each one of us will vary from person to person. But there's a danger that we get so tied up in knots about the pros and cons of one thing or another that we end up doing nothing. My encouragement to you is to do some research, choose your priorities, and then step out in faith.

A DAY IN THE LIFE[45]

With the sound of glass clinking on the doorstep, Sara knows the milkman has been. She drags herself downstairs, makes a strong Manumit coffee[46] and

---

45 Ok, so I'll admit that I've used a little bit of artistic licence to fit this all into one day. But you get the idea.

46 I couldn't resist giving a shout-out to Manumit Coffee Roasters, an ethical coffee-roasting company local to me in Cardiff, Wales, which trains and employs survivors of modern slavery. Find out more at manumitcoffee.co.uk.

reads her Bible before work. Sara's been in the Psalms recently, and this morning enjoyed meditating on Psalm 104, which marvels at the God of creation. If the Lord delights in sustaining his world (v 28-30), then that's the motivation she needs to get the flyers designed. Next Saturday it's the community litter-pick, and she agreed to get this month's advertising sent round her street's WhatsApp group.

She continues to be amazed at how many opportunities she's getting to talk with fellow litter-pickers about her faith. Sadly, the impression that several of her neighbours have picked up is that church people tend to be too other-worldly to get involved with such down-to-earth things, so Sara's enjoying being able to counter that idea. At the last count, three people had expressed an interest in coming to the forthcoming guest event at church.

Coffee downed. Check. Flyers designed. Check. She's about to hit print but realises they're just doing digital publicity this time.

Cereal poured. Cereal eaten. Check. Check. She's loving the new muesli that her colleague suggested from the zero-waste shop round the corner. Must start trying their new shampoo bars too. Apparently, they've got a fantastic new range, and someone from her church small group was raving about them.

Time to go! Sara fills her water bottle, turns off all the lights, jumps on her bike and races to work. She's looking forward to getting her teeth stuck into the new "green futures" project in the town-planning department, though she wishes her boss had heard Sunday's sermon about God being in control of the future. The way he goes on about the climate crisis ("We're all doomed!"), you'd have thought the sky was going to fall down tomorrow.

A discussion opens up over lunch about toilet paper, of all things. Two of Sara's colleagues swear by that new bamboo toilet paper, which comes plastic free. Someone else chimes in that since it's all imported from China, it's actually worse for the environment than bog-standard bog roll. Another pipes up that they're fed up with all the virtue signalling and that they could do without all this "middle-class guilt", thank you very much. Sara isn't quite sure what to think about this one but makes a mental note to pick the brains of her community litter-picking friends at the weekend, as well as her church small-group leader, who has taken an interest in the topic since attending a seminar at a Christian conference. There's nothing like thinking about this stuff with others!

The day continues. Mid-afternoon and Sara's really feeling that early start. Tempted to check out a little early, she's so glad that her younger sister designed that poster of 1 Corinthians 10 v 31 which hangs in pride of place behind the computer: "So whether you eat or drink or whatever you do, do it all for the glory of God". "Even sustainable town-planning, Lord?" Sara thinks to herself. But deep down she knows "whatever" means whatever and so gives it one last push.

And then it's home time. On Wednesday nights she hangs out with her brother's family, so Sara picks up *Planet Earth 2* on DVD (her nephews can't get enough of it!), a couple of takeaway pizzas and rings on the door. "Aunty Sara!" the twins explode with delight, and before you can say "Sir David Attenborough", the three of them have flopped in front of bright green ninja frogs fighting wasps in a Costa Rican jungle. Bliss.

The evening concludes with Sara singing the worship song "Indescribable" for the boys as she puts them both to bed. It's their favourite song, with good reason. As she sings of God placing and naming the stars in the sky, she means every word.

Sara finally heads home. Just time to swing past the polling booth at the nearby community centre. It's local elections day, and she's enjoyed grilling two of the candidates on how they plan on balancing long-term climate concerns with the short-term economic pressures. No easy answers there, but Sara's convinced it's been worth thinking about, as part of being a wise steward.

And then to bed. Sara's tired but full of joy after another day of prudent engagement with her

Father's world. But there's nothing like leaving it all in his sovereign hands as she finally nods off. See you tomorrow.

TAKING THINGS FURTHER

A Rocha International was founded by Peter and Miranda Harris. It is a global family of conservation organisations working together in response to the worldwide crisis of biodiversity loss, to carry out community-based conservation projects. They have loads of suggestions and resources on their website (http://arocha.org).

One of the most significant factors in carbon emissions is our use of energy. The Energy Saving Trust provides suggestions for how to make more efficient energy choices. Check out https://energysavingtrust.org.uk/top-10-energy-saving-actions-for-your-home/.

I've referred to the BBC's *Planet Earth* documentaries during this book, and if you've not seen them, I really would recommend them—they're spell-binding stuff. For a lower-budget but distinctly Christian equivalent, *The Riot and the Dance* video series by Gordon Wilson is a superb project. So far two documentaries have been made. Head to https://riotandthedance.com.

FOR YOUNGER ONES

The devotional books *Indescribable* and *How Great Is Our God* by Louie Giglio are excellent at capturing younger minds with the brilliance of God's amazing creation.

The movie *The Lorax,* based on the Dr Seuss children's book of the same name, is a good conversation starter for little ones about our use of the planet.

RESOURCES

- Dave Bookless, *Planetwise: Dare to Care for God's World* (IVP UK, 2008).
- Stephen Emmott, *10 Billion* (Penguin, 2013).
- Julian Hardyman, *Maximum Life: Living Every Day of Your Life for Jesus* (IVP UK, 2012).
- David Hegeman, *Plowing in Hope: Toward a Biblical Theology of Culture* (Canon Press, 2004).
- Louie Giglio, *Indescribable: 100 Devotions about God and Science* (Thomas Nelson, 2017) and *How Great Is Our God: 100 Indescribable Devotions about God and Science* (Thomas Nelson, 2020).
- Douglas J. Moo and Jonathan A. Moo, *Creation Care: A Biblical Theology of the Natural World* (Zondervan, 2018).
- Ian K. Smith, *Not Home Yet: How God's Renewal of the Earth Fits into God's Plan for the World* (Crossway, 2019).

- Greta Thunberg, *No One Is Too Small to Make a Difference* (Penguin, 2019).
- Lionel Windsor, *Is God Green?* (Matthias Media, 2018).
- Andrew Wilson, *God of All Things* (Zondervan, 2021).
- Gordon Wilson, *A Different Shade of Green: A Biblical Approach to Environmentalism and the Dominion Mandate* (Canon Press, 2019).
- Tom Wright, *Surprised by Hope* (SPCK, 2007).

ACKNOWLEDGEMENTS

It all started with a conversation about coffee cups. A couple of church members, Sarah and Anna, asked to talk with me about single-use plastics at church. We ended up discussing a whole range of green issues, and I remember conceding how green I was in my thinking, and not in the way they had hoped. That conversation got me thinking, and then reading, and then realising that if I was uninformed about the connection between the Bible and the environment, then the chances were that others would be too.

Once a year at Highfields Church, where I serve as pastor, we run a four-week seminar series entitled Equip, instead of our usual evening services. I find that forcing myself to teach on a topic is an excellent excuse to find out what I really think! With that recent conversation about the environment buzzing around my head, I decided to road-test my thoughts in a seminar track entitled "Is God Green?" shamelessly stealing the title from the helpful introduction to the topic by Lionel Windsor. I was also privileged to give the material a second outing at a couple of seminars at Word Alive 2022. I'm immensely grateful to everyone who attended those sessions, both at Highfields and in Prestatyn, and engaged with them so thoughtfully. I think I learnt as much as any from those times together.

Rachel Jones, from The Good Book Company, has been the first-time author's dream editor. Her questions, suggestions and general encouragement throughout the writing process have kept me on the straight and narrow and been invaluable throughout.

My children, Ella-Beth, Owen, Barney and Noah, have been the perfect support act in the writing of this book in everything from the enthusiastic ("How many words have you written today, Dad? Brilliant!") to the distracting ("What did you get in today's Wordle, Dad? We did it in three!"). And besides, their instinctive love and knowledge of the natural world simply blows me away. You bring such joy to life.

Lastly, what can I say about my wife, Sally? A constant and loving support, the nicest member of the grammar police one could possibly meet, and someone whose contagious wonder at the goodness, truth and beauty of God's creation has infected us all. It's to you that I dedicate this book, with immense gratitude to God.

Not to us, LORD, not to us
but to your name be the glory,
because of your love and faithfulness.

Psalm 115 v 1

THE ENVIRONMENT
DISCUSSION GUIDE

This series does not aim to say everything there is to say about a subject, but to give an overview and a solid grounding to how Christians should start to think about the issue from the Bible. We hope that as you discuss this book, and the Bible passages that it is based on, you will gain in confidence to speak faithfully, compassionately and wisely to others.

Below is an extensive list of questions. Please pick and choose the ones that suit your group and the time you have available. If you are leading a group, try to keep constantly in people's minds that this is not simply a discussion about a political or ethical "issue"—but that these are fears experienced by real people who are, perhaps, suffering deeply, and need our love and compassion, and, above all, the gospel message of hope.

TO START
- Where have you encountered conversations about the environment? What are some of the things you have heard or read recently?
- Before you started reading this book, what were some of the questions you had about the environment and green issues?
- Before you started reading this book, what were your thoughts about what the Christian view of the environment was or should be?

CHAPTER 1: GREETING GRETA
- How do you react to the list of bullet points on pages 15-17?

- Where on the "climate pendulum" do you find yourself most often?
- Have you experienced a situation where environmental issues have provided an opportunity for gospel witness?
- "The only thing that matters is evangelism." Have you encountered, or expressed, an objection similar to that? Having read this chapter, how would you now respond?
- How, practically, should we navigate the need to keep evangelism central without neglecting other important issues, such as creation care? Where have you seen this done well?

CHAPTER 2: MY FATHER'S WORLD

- What are some of your favourite things in the natural world that our Father has created?
- How would you sum up "the doctrine of creation"? How does that doctrine help us to avoid the extremes of panic and passivity on the "climate pendulum"?
- How would you sum up "the doctrine of sin"? How does that doctrine help us to avoid the extremes of panic and passivity on the "climate pendulum"?
- Which of the reasons from this chapter for Christians to care about the environment did you find most compelling? Can you think of any more?

CHAPTER 3: KINGS AND QUEENS OF NARNIA

- This chapter quoted David Attenborough as saying, "The future of humanity, and indeed of all life on Earth, now depends on us". Have you heard similar sentiments expressed in the past—and if so, how did they make you feel?

- What did you find most sobering, and most reassuring, in this chapter?
- Was there anything from the Bible in this chapter that was new to you or struck you afresh?
- What might it look like for us to "roll up our sleeves" as stewards of this world?

CHAPTER 4: TOMORROW NEVER DIES

- Is this world your home? Sum up the answer from this chapter.
- Was there anything in this chapter about the future of our planet that was new to you or which you have questions about?
- How does the idea that Jesus will renew our planet in the future motivate us to look after it today?
- Look at the four principles from pages 67-71 (regarding accountability, witness, timescales and continuity). Which of those do you think you are most likely to neglect or forget? How can you make sure that you keep it in view?
- What other principles from the book as a whole, or your own understanding of the Bible, could you add?

POSTSCRIPT

- What struck you from reading about a day in the life of Sara?
- What are some practical changes that you want to make in your own life to better care for creation?
- What areas do you still have questions about?
- What might it look like to engage with environmental issues as a church community?

TO FINISH

- What's the big thing that has impacted you from reading *The Environment*?
- How will you think about and pray for your friends, your neighbours and your government as they contemplate environmental issues?
- What extra help and information do you think you need to be more confident about what you believe on this subject?

PRAY

- Thank God for his bountiful creation. Ask him to help you understand environmental issues and the people they affect better.
- Pray that you and your church fellowship would take appropriate action in order to steward creation and love your neighbours well, for the glory of God.
- Pray for opportunities to share the hope of the gospel with non-Christian friends as you chat about this issue.
- Pray that the governments of the world would make wise policy decisions that work for the common good.

Printable copies of this discussion guide are available at:
www.thegoodbook.co.uk/talking-points-environment
www.thegoodbook.com/talking-points-environment

MORE TALKING POINTS BOOKS

TRANSGENDER

ABORTION

THE PORN PROBLEM

ASSISTED SUICIDE

thegoodbook
COMPANY

BIBLICAL | RELEVANT | ACCESSIBLE

At The Good Book Company, we are dedicated to helping Christians and local churches grow. We believe that God's growth process always starts with hearing clearly what he has said to us through his timeless word—the Bible.

Ever since we opened our doors in 1991, we have been striving to produce Bible-based resources that bring glory to God. We have grown to become an international provider of user-friendly resources to the Christian community, with believers of all backgrounds and denominations using our books, Bible studies, devotionals, evangelistic resources, and DVD-based courses.

We want to equip ordinary Christians to live for Christ day by day, and churches to grow in their knowledge of God, their love for one another, and the effectiveness of their outreach.

Call us for a discussion of your needs or visit one of our local websites for more information on the resources and services we provide.

Your friends at The Good Book Company

thegoodbook.com | thegoodbook.co.uk
thegoodbook.com.au | thegoodbook.co.nz
thegoodbook.co.in